The Real Book Multi-Tracks Vol. 12   For C, B♭, E♭ & Bass Clef Instruments

1950s JAZZ

Play-Along

T0081646

Trumpet: Jamie Breiwick
Tenor Sax: Jonathan Greenstein
Piano: Mark Davis
Bass: Jeff Hamann
Drums: David Bayles
Recorded by Ric Probst at Tanner-Monagle Studio

To access online content, visit:
www.halleonard.com/mylibrary

Enter Code
1538-9222-7397-9655

ISBN 978-1-5400-2637-8

For more information on the Real Book series, including community forums, please visit
www.OfficialRealBook.com

Visit Hal Leonard Online at
www.halleonard.com

Contact Us:
Hal Leonard
7777 West Bluemound Road
Milwaukee, WI 53213
Email: info@halleonard.com

In Europe contact:
Hal Leonard Europe Limited
42 Wigmore Street
Marylebone, London, W1U 2RN
Email: info@halleonardeurope.com

In Australia contact:
Hal Leonard Australia Pty. Ltd.
4 Lentara Court
Cheltenham, Victoria, 3192 Australia
Email: info@halleonard.com.au

Contents

DJANGO

— JOHN LEWIS

C VERSION

(SLOW & EVEN 8ths)

LAST X, RIT.   FINE

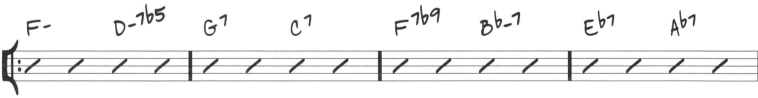

SOLOS (MED. SWING)

AFTER SOLOS, D.C. AL FINE

Doodlin'

(MED. SWING)

C VERSION

— HORACE SILVER

In Your Own Sweet Way

(MED. SWING)
C VERSION

- DAVE BRUBECK

FINE

AFTER SOLOS, D.S. AL FINE
(PLAY PICKUPS) (TAKE REPEAT)

JORDU

JERU

— Gerry Mulligan

C VERSION

(MED. SWING)

KILLER JOE

C VERSION
INTRO

- BENNY GOLSON

LULLABY OF BIRDLAND

— GEORGE DAVIS WEISS/GEORGE SHEARING

(MED.)

C VERSION

FINE   AFTER SOLOS, D.C. AL FINE
(TAKE REPEAT)

Night Train

- Oscar Washington/Lewis C. Simpkins/Jimmy Forrest

(MED. SWING)

C VERSION

WALTZ FOR DEBBY

— GENE LEES/BILL EVANS

C VERSION

AFTER SOLOS, D.C. AL ⊕

20

CON ALMA

— JOHN "DIZZY" GILLESPIE

(LATIN)

Bb VERSION

INTRO

DJANGO

— John Lewis

(SLOW 4 / EVEN 8ths)

Bb VERSION

SOLOS (MED. SWING)

LAST X, RIT.   FINE

AFTER SOLOS, D.C. AL FINE

In Your Own Sweet Way

(MED. SWING)

Bb VERSION

- DAVE BRUBECK

AFTER SOLOS, D.S. AL FINE
(PLAY PICKUPS) (TAKE REPEAT)

Jordu

JERU

— Gerry Mulligan

Killer Joe

- BENNY GOLSON

LULLABY OF BIRDLAND

(MED.)

– GEORGE DAVIS WEISS/GEORGE SHEARING

Bb VERSION

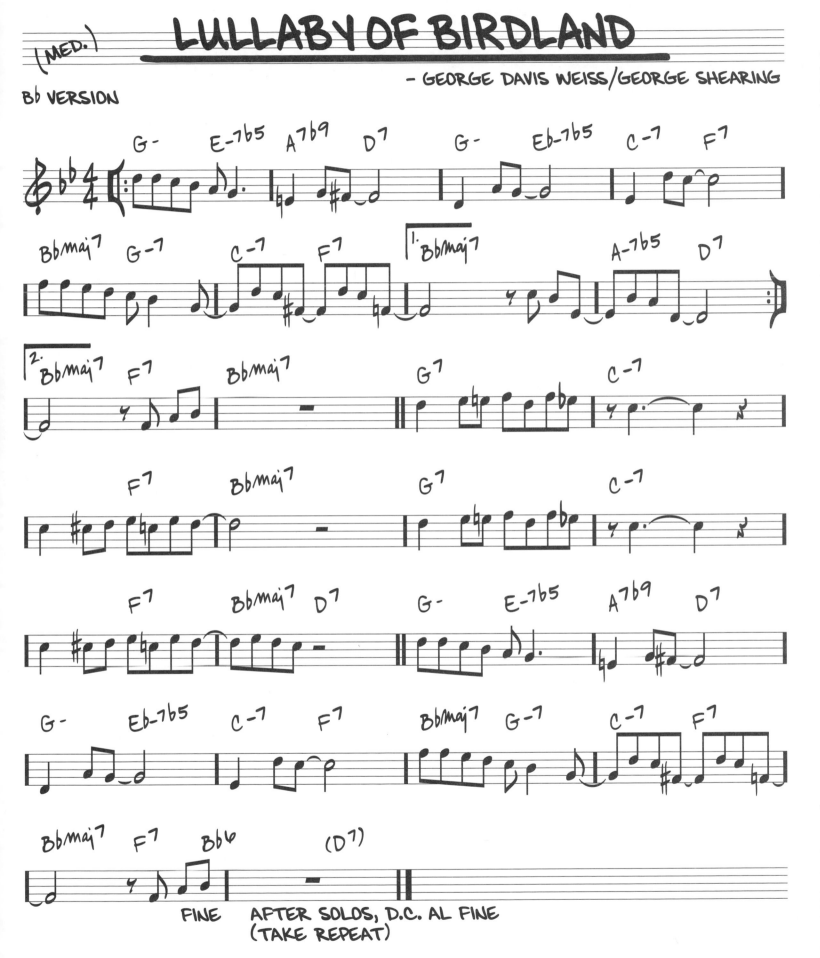

FINE   AFTER SOLOS, D.C. AL FINE
(TAKE REPEAT)

Night Train

- Oscar Washington/Lewis C. Simpkins/Jimmy Forrest

(MED. SWING)

Bb Version

WALTZ FOR DEBBY

— GENE LEES/BILL EVANS

CON ALMA

— JOHN "DIZZY" GILLESPIE

Eb VERSION
INTRO

DJANGO

— JOHN LEWIS

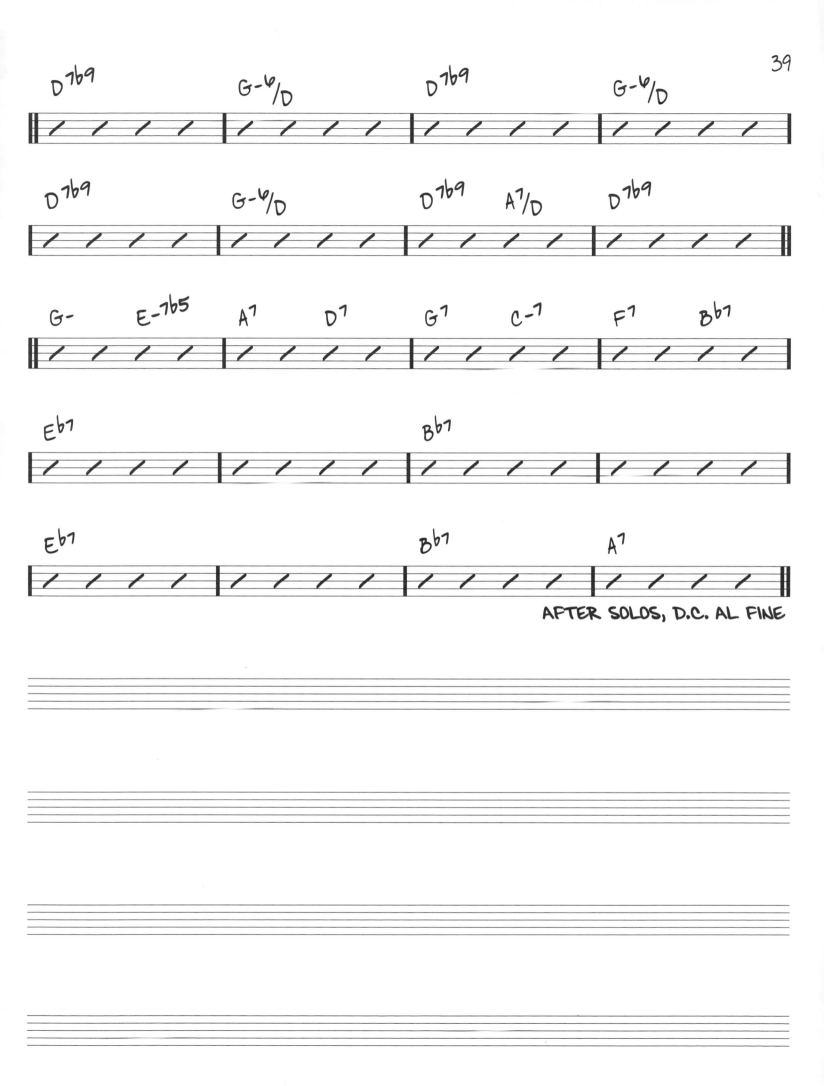

Doodlin'

(MED. SWING)

Eb Version

— Horace Silver

In Your Own Sweet Way

- Dave Brubeck

FINE
AFTER SOLOS, D.S. AL FINE
(PLAY PICKUPS) (TAKE REPEAT)

Jordu

JERU

- GERRY MULLIGAN

Killer Joe

Eb Version

– Benny Golson

LULLABY OF BIRDLAND

— GEORGE DAVIS WEISS/GEORGE SHEARING

FINE   AFTER SOLOS, D.C. AL FINE
(TAKE REPEAT)

Night Train

- Oscar Washington/Lewis C. Simpkins/Jimmy Forrest

WALTZ FOR DEBBY

— GENE LEES/BILL EVANS

Eb VERSION

Con Alma

— John "Dizzy" Gillespie

(LATIN)

⑨:C VERSION
INTRO

SOLOS ON [A] [A] [B] [A]
AFTER SOLOS, D.S. AL ⊕
(TAKE REPEAT)

DJANGO

— JOHN LEWIS

LAST X, RIT.   FINE

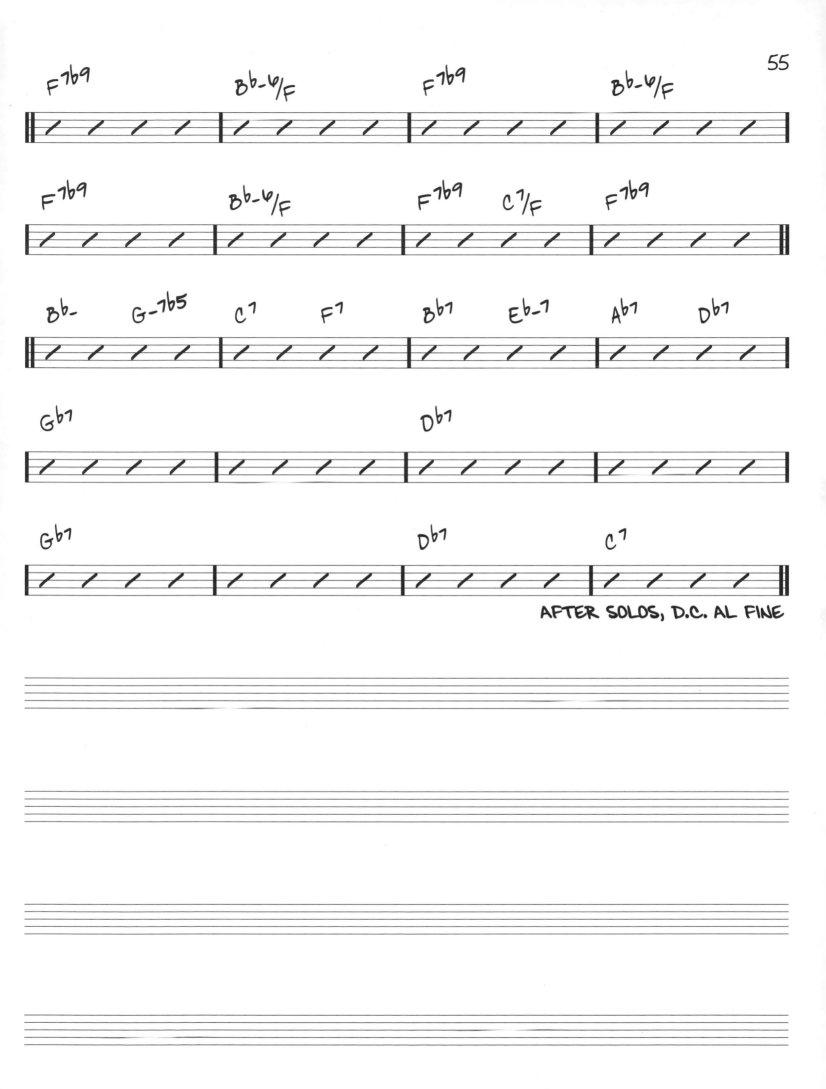

Doodlin'

(MED. SWING)

9: C VERSION

— Horace Silver

In Your Own Sweet Way

- Dave Brubeck

FINE
AFTER SOLOS, D.S. AL FINE
(PLAY PICKUPS) (TAKE REPEAT)

Jordu

JERU

— Gerry Mulligan

Killer Joe

- BENNY GOLSON

LULLABY OF BIRDLAND

— GEORGE DAVIS WEISS/GEORGE SHEARING

(MED.)

♪: C VERSION

FINE AFTER SOLOS, D.C. AL FINE
(TAKE REPEAT)

Night Train

- Oscar Washington/Lewis C. Simpkins/Jimmy Forrrest

WALTZ FOR DEBBY

— GENE LEES / BILL EVANS

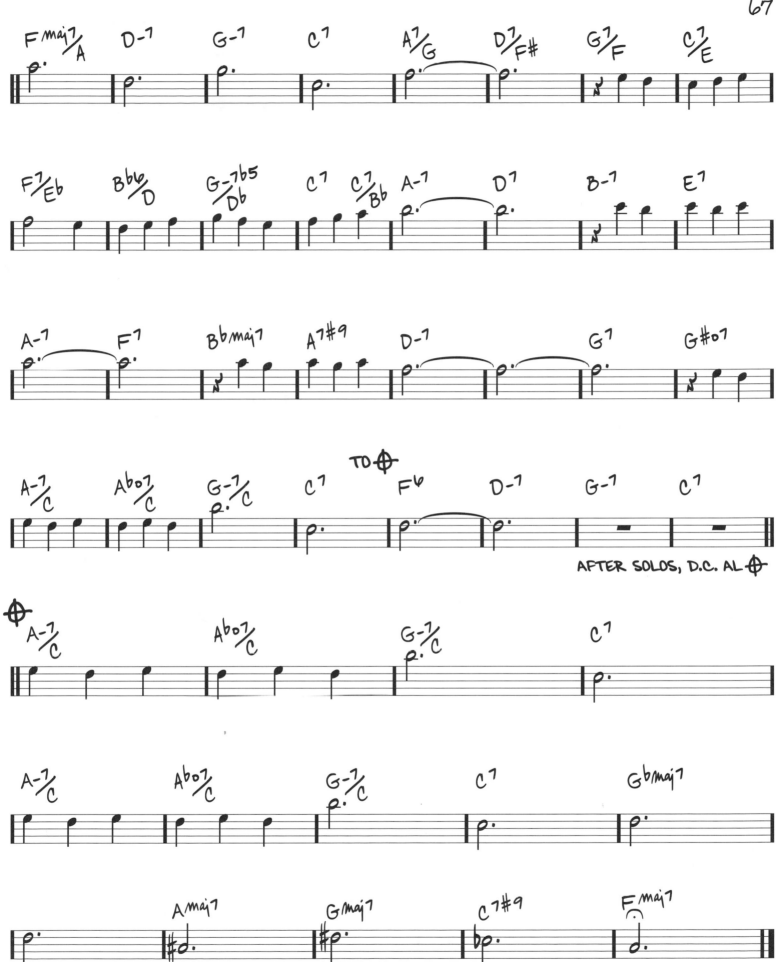

The Best-Selling Jazz Book of All Time Is Now Legal!

The Real Books are the most popular jazz books of all time. Since the 1970s, musicians have trusted these volumes to get them through every gig, night after night. The problem is that the books were illegally produced and distributed, without any regard to copyright law, or royalties paid to the composers who created these musical masterpieces.

Hal Leonard is very proud to present the first legitimate and legal editions of these books ever produced. You won't even notice the difference, other than all the notorious errors being fixed: the covers and typeface look the same, the song lists are nearly identical, and the price for our edition is even cheaper than the originals!

Every conscientious musician will appreciate that these books are now produced accurately and ethically, benefitting the songwriters that we owe for some of the greatest tunes of all time!

VOLUME 1
00240221	C Edition	$39.99
00240224	Bb Edition	$39.99
00240225	Eb Edition	$39.99
00240226	Bass Clef Edition	$39.99
00286389	F Edition	$39.99
00240292	C Edition 6 x 9	$35.00
00240339	Bb Edition 6 x 9	$35.00
00147792	Bass Clef Edition 6 x 9	$35.00
00451087	C Edition on CD-ROM	$29.99
00200984	Online Backing Tracks: Selections	$45.00
00110604	Book/USB Flash Drive Backing Tracks Pack	$79.99
00110599	USB Flash Drive Only	$50.00

VOLUME 2
00240222	C Edition	$39.99
00240227	Bb Edition	$39.99
00240228	Eb Edition	$39.99
00240229	Bass Clef Edition	$39.99
00240293	C Edition 6 x 9	$35.00
00125900	Bb Edition 6 x 9	$35.00
00451088	C Edition on CD-ROM	$30.99
00125900	The Real Book – Mini Edition	$35.00
00204126	Backing Tracks on USB Flash Drive	$50.00
00204131	C Edition – USB Flash Drive Pack	$79.99

VOLUME 3
00240233	C Edition	$39.99
00240284	Bb Edition	$39.99
00240285	Eb Edition	$39.99
00240286	Bass Clef Edition	$39.99
00240338	C Edition 6 x 9	$35.00
00451089	C Edition on CD-ROM	$29.99

VOLUME 4
00240296	C Edition	$39.99
00103348	Bb Edition	$39.99
00103349	Eb Edition	$39.99
00103350	Bass Clef Edition	$39.99

VOLUME 5
00240349	C Edition	$39.99
00175278	Bb Edition	$39.99
00175279	Eb Edition	$39.99

VOLUME 6
00240534	C Edition	$39.99
00223637	Eb Edition	$39.99

Also available:
00154230	The Real Bebop Book	$34.99
00240264	The Real Blues Book	$34.99
00310910	The Real Bluegrass Book	$35.00
00240223	The Real Broadway Book	$35.00
00240440	The Trane Book	$22.99
00125426	The Real Country Book	$39.99
00269721	The Real Miles Davis Book C Edition	$24.99
00269723	The Real Miles Davis Book Bb Edition	$24.99
00240355	The Real Dixieland Book C Edition	$32.50
00294853	The Real Dixieland Book Eb Edition	$35.00
00122335	The Real Dixieland Book Bb Edition	$35.00
00240235	The Duke Ellington Real Book	$22.99
00240268	The Real Jazz Solos Book	$30.00
00240348	The Real Latin Book C Edition	$37.50
00127107	The Real Latin Book Bb Edition	$35.00
00120809	The Pat Metheny Real Book C Edition	$27.50
00252119	The Pat Metheny Real Book Bb Edition	$24.99
00240358	The Charlie Parker Real Book C Edition	$19.99
00275997	The Charlie Parker Real Book Eb Edition	$19.99
00118324	The Real Pop Book – Vol. 1	$35.00
00240331	The Bud Powell Real Book	$19.99
00240437	The Real R&B Book C Edition	$39.99
00276590	The Real R&B Book Bb Edition	$39.99
00240313	The Real Rock Book	$35.00
00240323	The Real Rock Book – Vol. 2	$35.00
00240359	The Real Tab Book	$32.50
00240317	The Real Worship Book	$29.99

THE REAL CHRISTMAS BOOK
00240306	C Edition	$32.50
00240345	Bb Edition	$32.50
00240346	Eb Edition	$35.00
00240347	Bass Clef Edition	$32.50
00240431	A-G CD Backing Tracks	$24.99
00240432	H-M CD Backing Tracks	$24.99
00240433	N-Y CD Backing Tracks	$24.99

THE REAL VOCAL BOOK
00240230	Volume 1 High Voice	$35.00
00240307	Volume 1 Low Voice	$35.00
00240231	Volume 2 High Voice	$35.00
00240308	Volume 2 Low Voice	$35.00
00240391	Volume 3 High Voice	$35.00
00240392	Volume 3 Low Voice	$35.00
00118318	Volume 4 High Voice	$35.00
00118319	Volume 4 Low Voice	$35.00

Complete song lists online at www.halleonard.com

Prices, content, and availability subject to change without notice.

0719
318

THE REAL BOOK MULTI-TRACKS

TODAY'S BEST WAY TO PRACTICE JAZZ! Accurate, easy-to-read lead sheets and professional, customizable audio tracks accessed online for 10 songs

1. MAIDEN VOYAGE PLAY-ALONG

Autumn Leaves • Blue Bossa • Doxy • Footprints • Maiden Voyage • Now's the Time • On Green Dolphin Street • Satin Doll • Summertime • Tune Up.
00196616 Book with Online Media...........$17.99

2. MILES DAVIS PLAY-ALONG

Blue in Green • Boplicity (Be Bop Lives) • Four • Freddie Freeloader • Milestones • Nardis • Seven Steps to Heaven • So What • Solar • Walkin'.
00196798 Book with Online Media $17.99

3. ALL BLUES PLAY-ALONG

All Blues • Back at the Chicken Shack • Billic's Bounce (Bill's Bounce) • Birk's Works • Blues by Five • C-Jam Blues • Mr. P.C. • One for Daddy-O • Reunion Blues • Turnaround.
00196692 Book with Online Media $17.99

4. CHARLIE PARKER PLAY-ALONG

Anthropology • Blues for Alice • Confirmation • Donna Lee • K.C. Blues • Moose the Mooche • My Little Suede Shoes • Ornithology • Scrapple from the Apple • Yardbird Suite.
00196799 Book with Online Media $17.99

5. JAZZ FUNK PLAY-ALONG

Alligator Bogaloo • The Chicken • Cissy Strut • Cold Duck Time • Comin' Home Baby • Mercy, Mercy, Mercy • Put It Where You Want It • Sidewinder • Tom Cat • Watermelon Man.
00196728 Book with Online Media $17.99

6. SONNY ROLLINS PLAY-ALONG

Airegin • Blue Seven • Doxy • Duke of Iron • Oleo • Pent up House • St. Thomas • Sonnymoon for Two • Strode Rode • Tenor Madness.
00218264 Book with Online Media $17.99

7. THELONIOUS MONK PLAY-ALONG

Bemsha Swing • Blue Monk • Bright Mississippi • Green Chimneys • Monk's Dream • Reflections • Rhythm-a-ning • 'Round Midnight • Straight No Chaser • Ugly Beauty.
00232768 Book with Online Media $17.99

8. BEBOP ERA PLAY-ALONG

Au Privave • Boneology • Bouncing with Bud • Dexterity • Groovin' High • Half Nelson • In Walked Bud • Lady Bird • Move • Witches Pit.
00196728 Book with Online Media $17.99

9. CHRISTMAS CLASSICS PLAY-ALONG

Blue Christmas • Christmas Time Is Here • Frosty the Snow Man • Have Yourself a Merry Little Christmas • I'll Be Home for Christmas • My Favorite Things • Santa Claus Is Comin' to Town • Silver Bells • White Christmas • Winter Wonderland.
00236808 Book with Online Media..........$17.99

10. CHRISTMAS SONGS PLAY-ALONG

Away in a Manger • The First Noel • Go, Tell It on the Mountain • Hark! the Herald Angels Sing • Jingle Bells • Joy to the World • O Come, All Ye Faithful • O Holy Night • Up on the Housetop • We Wish You a Merry Christmas.
00236809 Book with Online Media..........$17.99

11. JOHN COLTRANE PLAY-ALONG

Blue Train (Blue Trane) • Central Park West • Cousin Mary • Giant Steps • Impressions • Lazy Bird • Moment's Notice • My Favorite Things • Naima (Niema) • Syeeda's Song Flute.
00275624 Book with Online Media $17.99

12. 1950S JAZZ PLAY-ALONG

Con Alma • Django • Doodlin' • In Your Own Sweet Way • Jeru • Jordu • Killer Joe • Lullaby of Birdland • Night Train • Waltz for Debby.
00275647 Book with Online Media $17.99

13. 1960S JAZZ PLAY-ALONG

Ceora • Dat Dere • Dolphin Dance • Equinox • Jeannine • Recorda Me • Stolen Moments • Tom Thumb • Up Jumped Spring • Windows.
00275651 Book with Online Media $17.99

14. 1970S JAZZ PLAY-ALONG

Birdland • Bolivia • Chameleon • 500 Miles High • Lucky Southern • Phase Dance • Red Baron • Red Clay • Spain • Sugar.
00275652 Book with Online Media........$17.99

15. CHRISTMAS TUNES PLAY-ALONG

The Christmas Song (Chestnuts Roasting on an Open Fire) • Do You Hear What I Hear • Feliz Navidad • Here Comes Santa Claus (Right down Santa Claus Lane) • A Holly Jolly Christmas • Let It Snow! Let It Snow! Let It Snow! • The Little Drummer Boy • The Most Wonderful Time of the Year • Rudolph the Red-Nosed Reindeer • Sleigh Ride.
00278073 Book with Online Media $17.99